WHAT'S REALLY IMPORTANT

By Brett Ledbetter

Printed in the United States of America.

Books may be purchased in quantity and/or special sales by contacting What Drives Winning at info@whatdriveswinning.com or visiting WhatDrivesWinning.com.

Library of Congress In-Publication data has been applied for.

ISBN: 978-0-9962264-7-9

Cover and interior design by Lisa Kuntz

FIRST EDITION

10 9 8 7 6 5 4 3 2 1

THE IDEAS IN THIS BOOK INSPIRED...

WHAT DRIVES WINNING

2018 CONFERENCE

Learn more at 2018.WhatDrivesWinning.com

TABLE OF CONTENTS

A Special Thank-You:
To all the coaches who have shared their thoughts and helped shape my thinking around this book.

WHAT'S REALLY IMPORTANT

PROLOGUE:
"I NEEDED TO BE GREAT"

"I Needed to Be Great"

Why do you think a lot of coaches I've worked with experience a level of depression after winning a national championship?

Consider this story:

A coach in his mid-forties won his first national championship.

After winning it, something came over him, and he went to a dark place.

Why?

It was the first time he could assess: Was it worth it?

It took twenty years for him to be able to make that assessment.

And now that he was there, he could finally run the cost-benefit analysis.

I asked him, "What did you sacrifice to get there?"

His eyes welled up. "Everything."

He started to unpack what that answer meant. And as he broke down his answer, it became clear.

His actions communicated to everyone who mattered most to him a simple message: What I'm chasing is more important than you.

His obsession to achieve created a distance in his marriage and an absence with his kids.

As we were talking he paused, and with regret, he said to me, "I needed to be great."

His solemn facial expression communicated the pain that existed behind that statement.

There were twenty years of actions that couldn't be reversed.

The more I'm around championship coaches, the more I realize there are some circumstances where instead of staging celebrations for championships, we should be staging interventions.

That conversation, along with many others that will follow in this book, has shaped my thinking around how to prioritize what's really important.

Is There a Cost to Greatness?

Is There a Cost to Greatness?

One of my favorite scenes that I like to show coaches comes from the movie *Whiplash*.

The scene features a young drummer named Andrew.

Andrew has decided that he needs to clear the way for greatness.

To him, that means he needs to break up with his girl-friend, Nicole.

Here's how Andrew delivers the news to her:

"I don't think we should be together.

And I've thought about it a lot, and this is what's going to happen.

I'm going to keep pursuing what I'm pursuing.

And because I'm doing that it's going to take up more and more of my time, and I'm not going to be able to spend as much time with you.

And even when I do spend time with you, I'm going to be thinking about drumming.

And I'm going to be thinking about jazz music and my charts and all that.

And because of that you're going to start to resent me.

And you're going to tell me to ease up on the drumming and spend more time with you, because you're not feeling important.

And I'm not going to be able to do that.

And really I'm just going to resent you for even asking me to stop drumming.

And we're just going to start to hate each other.

And it's going to get very—it's going to be ugly.

So for those reasons, I'd rather just break it off clean.

(pause)

Because I want to be great."

As that clip ends, I ask coaches, "How many of you can relate to what Andrew said?"

That question usually divides the room.

Some agree with Andrew's perspective. Others don't.

Either way, it starts the conversation about the cost of greatness. We begin by asking two questions.

THE QUADRANT

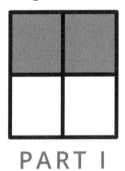

PART I

Question One:
What have you sacrificed to chase greatness?

1.

2.

3.

4.

5.

Question Two:
Why do you sacrifice so much?

1.

2.

3.

4.

5.

The Quadrant

When I work with high-achieving coaches, I hand them a sheet of paper.

I then ask them to draw two lines to form a quadrant.

It should look like this:

Once we have the quadrant, we jump in to part one.

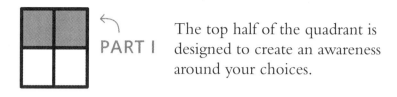

PART I   The top half of the quadrant is designed to create an awareness around your choices.

Here's how we begin that conversation.

 Exercise I: What Have You Sacrificed?

We start in the top left section with a one-minute exercise.

I ask the coaches I work with to write out in bullet-point form their answers to this question:

What have you sacrificed to chase greatness?

Here are the most common answers I see:

Time with Loved Ones
Family Events (Weddings, Funerals, Birthdays, Vacations)
Health (Mental, Emotional, Physical)
Social Life
Personal Time
Sleep
Self-Care

Take a second to think. Can you relate to these answers?

We'll circle back to this list after we finish the next exercise.

⊞ Exercise II: Why Do You Sacrifice?

In the top right section, we do another one-minute exercise.

I ask them to write down in bullet-point form their answers to this question:

Why do you sacrifice so much?

Here are the most common answers I see:

> Win
> Desire to Be Great
> Passion for the Job
> Fear of Failure
> Don't Want to Be Outworked
> Prove Myself
> The Pursuit Is Thrilling
> Take Program to Next Level

As you look at this list, take a second to think.

Do any of these answers resonate with you?

Now that the coaches can see their responses on paper, we perform a cost-benefit analysis.

Choice Awareness

Observe this coach's choices (on the next page).

What do you sacrifice?	Why do you sacrifice?
Time with Loved Ones	Win
Family Events	Desire to Be Great
Health	Passion for the Job
Social Life	Fear of Failure
Personal Time	Don't Want to Be Outworked
Sleep	Prove Myself
Self-Care	The Pursuit Is Thrilling
Stability	Take Program to Next Level

We're able to see <u>what</u> this coach is willing to sacrifice on the left.

And <u>why</u> they sacrifice on the right.

If you were observing this coach's choices, what would you think?

Would you have a positive or negative viewpoint?

This question usually divides the room into two perspectives.

One perspective will say, "This person has a successful mindset. They're driven. They're committed. They're dedicated. They'll do what it takes to get it done."

The other perspective will say, "Can't get that time back. Blind dedication has collateral damage. If this person doesn't shift their priorities, it's going to end in a crash."

A coach once asked me, "Is this supposed to make me feel like shit?"

The goal of this exercise is not to make you feel bad.

The goal is to create an awareness around your choices.

Before we move on to the bottom half of the quadrant, I'd like to introduce you to two people: Mike Holder and Mary Wise.

MIKE HOLDER
Athletic Director: Oklahoma State

Meet Mike Holder

Mike Holder has transitioned from an iconic golf coach at Oklahoma State University to being the athletic director.

As a coach, he won nine national championships.

That's on top of raising $31 million dollars to build the state-of-the-art golf course facility Karsten Creek.

"Karsten" helped Mike attract the best talent away from other high-performing, pleasant-weather universities.

That speaks to his innovation.

Despite winning nine national championships, Mike will say, "I left a few on the table."

When you ask, "Why do you say that?"

He'll say, "I made it too hard. I took a lot of the fun out of it."

That's one of his regrets, but not the biggest.

"Leaving a few on the table" pales in comparison to some of his other regrets.

Mike's favorite quote is, "If youth knew. If age could."

If he had the wisdom that he has today, he would have done things differently when he started coaching at 22 years old.

If Youth Knew...

When it comes to championships, Mike said that he would tell his younger self, "Don't place too much significance in them."

He was guilty of that, acknowledging that he placed too much importance on:

How well you played
How low your round was
How many championships you won

Upon reflection, Mike said, "In life, those things mean nothing."

He would have changed his priorities to:

Did you feel joy while you were preparing?
Did you look forward to every day?
Did you have someone that could help you enjoy it?

For the majority of his career, he said, "I was in the wrong place with the wrong priorities and the wrong mindset."

What does that place look like?

Mike said, "It's a place where the only joy is for the ultimate achievement. And then when you get it, it's gone in an instant, and what's left?"

That shows how fleeting success is.

It's easy to get on that channel.

For Mike, he said, "I had a burning desire to be great at something."

He wasn't a great golfer, but he worked at it.

It was a natural progression for him to go into coaching and continue to chase greatness.

He had something to prove when he entered coaching.

As a young coach, Mike thought, "The score was everything."

Now, he says, "There was a cost that went along with it. I recognize that now."

What Was the Cost?

Mike started to recognize the cost of excellence when his daughter was around 12 years old.

He gets misty-eyed when he talks about it.

If he could go back to tell his younger self something, he would say, "That daughter of yours is a whole lot more important than you are, and you need to understand that."

He continued, "Her hopes, dreams, aspirations, and future are a lot more important than what you want for yourself or the view you have for yourself. You need to accept that."

The question is: Would his younger self have listened?

The younger Mike Holder wouldn't have heard the older Mike Holder.

The younger Mike Holder had to touch the stove to see if it was hot.

He needed to learn through experience despite the collateral damage.

That need was brought to light on a walk that I had with him.

It was a chilling experience.

It felt like I was speaking to an older version of myself.

I asked him, "If you could go back and do it all over again—would you change it?"

He answered with five words.

He said, "I **needed** to be great."

I deeply empathized with what he was saying.

When he was younger, he didn't have the perspective to understand what was important in the long run.

He was caught in a phase where he needed to prove something.

When you need to prove something, it usually comes from a place of *I'm not good enough.*

That insecurity can blind you from some of life's best offerings.

But it also provides a deep reservoir of energy that can give you the capacity to accomplish amazing things.

The cost?

Eventually you'll have to deal with what you've neglected.

Mike's view on that is clear.

He's come to peace with himself, saying, "Without knowing what I know now, if you put me back in the same circumstance, I'd repeat a lot of the same."

Mike had to earn his wisdom the hard way, which demonstrates why this quote means so much to him:

"If youth knew. If age could."

If Youth Knew...

**What are the top five things you know now
that you would tell your younger self?**

1.

2.

3.

4.

5.

**Would your younger self
have listened to that advice?**

We asked coaches across the country:

What are the top five things you know now that you would tell your younger self?

Here are some of their answers:

"Don't overvalue the outcome. If you do, you will live and die a miserable person."

"Fulfillment doesn't reside in achievement."

"Refine your motives for coaching—it's not about you."

"Don't take losing out on the people who love you most."

"Your greatest contribution will be the human development—not sport development—of your athletes."

"The drug of helping people can lead to the closest people in your life resenting you if not balanced properly."

"More work isn't always the answer."

"Realize that you can't save everyone. Your job is to plant and water seeds through creating awareness."

"Don't expect everyone to want it like you."

"When you start to feel cynical, you need to take a break to gain perspective."

"Your responses to events determine the long-term trajectory of your path. Work on them."

"Criticism never goes away, no matter how much success you have."

"Your need to prove yourself can wreck your life."

"Figure out what to ignore. You don't get the time back that you spend on things that don't matter."

"You are a product of what the people around you reinforce. Don't find yourself through their approval."

"Prioritize growth and service—it will help prepare you for everything."

"Invest your time into things that are lasting and real."

"Your emotional reactions communicate a value system. Regulate those reactions."

"Monitor your question-to-statement ratio. Ask more questions."

"Contrary to what you think, you don't know everything."

"Don't destroy your life for a finish line that doesn't exist."

MARY WISE

Volleyball: Florida

Did I Fail?

Take a look at this resume:

89% Winning Percentage
23 SEC Championships
8 Final Fours
40 All-Americans

When you see that list of achievements, what do you think?

Pretty impressive, right?

Here's a question for you: Is it possible to feel like you've failed with this resume?

Mary Wise will say it is.

How does she know?

She's lived it—that's her resume.

So how does that happen?

The University of Florida has a roster of championship coaches that set the bar high when it comes to achievement.

This creates a unique norm.

Mary said, "If winning the championship is the norm, you can get caught up in that."

What does it look like to 'get caught up in that?'

It's thinking that anything less than a championship isn't good enough.

For twenty years, that obsession to achieve drove Mary's life.

And she admits that she could hear other people tell her, "That's the wrong way to look at it."

She couldn't buy it.

It didn't matter who the source was.

Mary sat down with Billy Donovan, head basketball coach at the University of Florida at that time.

In 2006 and 2007, Billy won back-to-back national championships.

Mary said to him about the championship, "I want so badly to win it."

To which Billy responded, "You think that will change you, it will not. You'll be working just as hard to get back there."

The seed was planted, but her actions didn't change.

Why couldn't Mary hear Billy?

She kept seeing something else.

Mary kept seeing her colleagues raise national championship trophies.

That created the feeling, "I'm not equal until I win one."

Mary needed the trophy to validate her.

She attached her importance to achievement, and her environment kept reinforcing that.

Here's an example of that in action.

Championship Cues

In 2017, the University of Florida volleyball program had an unbelievable year.

It was arguably the best in Mary's career.

Mary won AVCA Coach of the Year, and her team competed in the national championship game, where they fell to Nebraska.

A week later, Mary and her husband were waiting out-side of a restaurant in Gainesville, Florida.

An older man walked by and made eye contact with Mary.

Mary recalled, "You could tell he recognized me."

He approached her with an enthusiastic, "Hey!"

But then he remembered they lost in the national championship.

And he disappointedly said to Mary, "Oh…that match. That was really rough."

Then, he just walked away.

What can we learn from that?

The environment Mary lives in is constantly sending her cues.

It'd be easy to internalize those cues as, "Win it all, or the season is a disappointment."

Young Mary internalized those signals.

Meet Young Mary

Perspective is something Young Mary didn't have.

Mary said, "Young Mary had horse blinders on."

She obsessed over the win / loss column.

Mary reflected, "I was this weak: After a loss, I didn't even want to be seen in public."

She didn't want people looking at her saying, "She should be watching videotape because her team lost."

Mary acknowledged, "I'm certain that's just ego-driven."

For twenty years, she maniacally prioritized her job and doing what it takes to get it done.

Young Mary overvalued achievement and undervalued growth and relationships.

The more experienced Mary has a refined perspective.

The experienced Mary loves this quote by Barbara Bush:

"At the end of your life you will never regret not having passed one more test, not winning one more verdict, or not closing one more deal. You will regret time not spent with a husband, a friend, a child, or a parent."

I asked Mary, "What would have happened if you had given that quote to Young Mary?"

"Young Mary would have said, 'You'll work hard enough. You're good enough. You can still make that phone call *and* still be a good mom,'" Mary said.

"That was ego-driven."

If Youth Knew...

If you ask the more experienced Mary, "Would a championship validate your career?"

She can honestly answer, "No."

The more experienced Mary knows what's important.

I asked her to write a letter to Young Mary to see what she would tell her.

Here's what she wrote:

Dear Young Mary:

I know that you're judged by that win/loss column.

You're hired and fired by it.

But you must believe there's something more important than that.

And that belief must be part of your core.

Because when it is, you'll have perspective to help you get over the losses. (That doesn't mean losing becomes easy—it never does.)

But you can have some perspective.

That's the one thing that I wish I could give you. Perspective.

And I encourage you to seek that earlier.

It will help you direct your energy at what's important, and your players will appreciate that.

They'll appreciate seeing that there are more important things to you…than just winning.

If they feel like winning is the most important thing, they'll start to internalize they are only important to a coach if they are successful.

You don't want them to feel that way.

Take it from me, I know what that feels like to have your importance be attached to your achievement.

And you don't want to feel that for the next 20 years.

Seek perspective.

Love,
Mary Wise

There's wisdom in that advice.

Mary's earned that perspective.

So how do you begin the conversation around what's really important?

That's where we'll head next.

THE QUADRANT

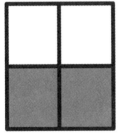

PART II

Society Scorecard
How does society measure your success as a coach?

1.

2.

3.

4.

5.

Dr. Jim Loehr introduced me to the idea of a Society Scorecard. You can learn more in his book The Only Way To Win.

What's Important to You?
Answer this question ten times
(It's geared at life in general.)

1.

2.

3.

4.

5.

6.

7.

8.

9.

10.

Rank your top five in order.

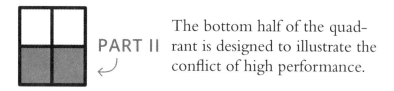

PART II   The bottom half of the quadrant is designed to illustrate the conflict of high performance.

Here's how we begin that conversation.

Exercise III: Society Scorecard

In the bottom right section, I ask the coaches I work with to write out in bullet-point form the answer to this question:

How does society measure your success *as a coach*?

I ask them to give me their top five. Here are the most common answers I see:

Win/Loss Record
Championships
Rankings
Players at Next Level
Rivalry Games

Take a look at these answers. Do any of them apply to you?

We'll come back to these answers in a second. Before we do, let's move to the last exercise in the quadrant.

⊞ Exercise IV: What's Important to You?

In the bottom left section, I ask coaches to answer one question, TEN times.

The question is, "What's important to you?" It's geared at life in general.

When I do this with a coach, I'll ask the question, "What's important to you?"

They'll write down the first thing that comes to mind.

I'll ask the same question again.

They'll write the next thing that comes to mind.

And we do that until we get ten answers.

There's a rhythm that develops with the exercise.

Here's an example from a coach I was working with:

What's important to you?
Family

What's important to you?
Faith

What's important to you?
Strong character

What's important to you?
Job performance

What's important to you?
Health

What's important to you?
Friends

What's important to you?
Relationships

What's important to you?
Financial security

What's important to you?
Turning boys into men

What's important to you?
My staff

Can you relate to some of his answers?

Here's what we do once we finish.

I asked him to look at his list to see if there was anything that he left off.

After he had a few seconds to look, I asked him to rank his top five.

Here they are:

> Faith
> Family
> Health
> Strong Character
> Relationships

I asked him to compare his top five values to the Society Scorecard.

Here they are side by side:

What's Important?	Society Scorecard
Faith	Win/Loss Record
Family	Championships
Health	Rankings
Strong Character	Players at Next Level
Relationships	Rivalry Games

During this exercise, I ask the coaches I work with, "What do you think about these two lists?"

They say, "There's not a lot of crossover."

I ask them, "What do you think about that?"

They respond with something like, "It's clear that my values are different than society's."

That awareness can create conflict.

Especially when you realize that everyone around you is reinforcing behavior that can directly undermine what's important to you.

For most people, the more you achieve, the harder it can be to maintain proper perspective.

Let's learn from someone who's traveled that path.

Meet Urban Meyer.

URBAN MEYER

Football: Ohio State

The Search

When I first met with Urban Meyer, I showed him a speech that Jim Carrey gave at the 2016 Golden Globes.

Here's what Jim Carrey said:

"I am two-time Golden Globe winner, Jim Carrey.

When I go to sleep at night, I'm not just a guy going to sleep.

I'm two-time Golden Globe winner, Jim Carrey, going to get some well-needed shut-eye.

And when I dream, I don't just dream any old dream.

No sir.

I dream about being three-time Golden Globe winning actor, Jim Carrey.

Because…then I would be enough.

It would finally be true.

And I could stop this terrible search for what I know ultimately won't fulfill me.

But these are important, these awards.

I don't want you to think that just because if you blew up our solar system alone, you wouldn't be able to find us, or any of human history with the naked eye.

But from our perspective…this is huge."

After Urban watched it, he smiled. "Two-time Golden Globe winner," he said, "It is really important."

But then, Urban said, "Deep down, how important is it really? You know, in the big picture of things?"

That's the conflict of high-performance: what's important versus what's really important.

What's Important vs What's *Really* Important

When you ask Urban about his father, he'll say, "He had the same beliefs I have. Family was so important."

To try to gain insight into how Urban was socialized, I asked him, "When was your father most proud of you?"

After a second, he responded, "Either an athletic achievement or a coaching achievement."

Urban's socialization revolved around two things: strong family values and the reinforcement of achievement.

That's ultimately what created tension in his life.

He grew up two hours away from where he now coaches.

At that time, Woody Hayes was the head football coach of The Ohio State Buckeyes.

Urban was raised on Woody's mentality: "The hardest-working person (or team) will win."

When you combine that mentality with clinical levels of focus, predictable events usually occur.

I Became the Man I Didn't Want to Be

Urban said that while coaching at Florida, "Everything was focused on winning that championship."

He continued, "When I'm getting up in the morning, when I'm playing golf, when I'm with my family, I'm thinking about 'How do we get to that championship?'"

That obsession to achieve wrecked Urban's life.

When do you realize you're off track?

"When you start putting the things that mean the most to you aside," Urban said.

When you take family, faith, and health out of your schedule, bad things happen.

Urban acknowledged, "I'm the poster child for that."

He became consumed. When that happens, there are life events that help wake you up.

Here's what woke him up:

He attended his daughter's National Letter of Intent signing to play college volleyball. She gave a speech.

He recalled what she said: "Mom, you were always there. Dad, I love you. You were great. But you *weren't* always there."

As Urban sat in the audience, he felt guilt.

"That's where it hit home that I became the guy that I didn't want to be," Urban said. "I have a couple trophies on the wall, but I missed a lot of what's really important."

The 10-Year Sprint

Urban said, "I was going to write a book at one point. I was going to call it *The 10-Year Sprint.*"

That book would be about perfection.

When you become consumed with perfection, you lose perspective.

When you lose perspective, things become bigger than they are.

Urban said, "The loss of a game was like you weren't going to see tomorrow."

Everybody around him felt that.

He thought, *If I can just get it to this level, things will get easier.*

Urban did get it to *that* level.

And it didn't get easier.

He learned a lot from his first championship experience.

Urban said, "When you hit the pinnacle, you expect things to change, and they don't. They just get a little more complicated."

Which leads to confusion.

Urban recalled sitting in the locker room after winning his first national championship.

He thought, "Now we're playing with house money. Now I get to coach for fun, and this is going to be a walk in the park from this point forward."

"And obviously, it's not true." he said.

To reach the pinnacle, Urban realized the energy investment that it required.

When you reach it, he said, "You wanted to take a deep breath. And you wanted to take a couple months off."

But that's not what happens.

Urban said, "The next day you're on the road recruiting."

Hence the title of the book Urban never wrote: *The 10-Year Sprint.*

The more you achieve, the faster the treadmill becomes in order to maintain the expectation level that your performance set.

Pretty soon, you realize your life is a sprint.

Building and Sustaining Are Different

Consider this quote from Urban:

"The energy and thrill to climb the mountain is awesome. To maintain that is nothing but fatigue."

What does that mean?

When you're climbing the mountain, progress is happening.

You're at a higher place than you were before.

People can see that progression, and that ignites excitement in everyone around you because you're in new territory.

But when you reach the top of the mountain, you can't go higher. All you can do is repeat.

However, this time you have the knowledge of how hard that climb is...before it starts.

There's not a lot of joy inside the job if it becomes an all-or-nothing situation.

What does that look like?

Either you win the championship, and you did what you were supposed to do.

–or–

You didn't, and the season was a disappointment.

When your achievement has led to *Home of the National Champions* being written above the press box, there's a good chance you're living with an all-or-nothing fanbase.

"You create this beast," Urban said. "And unfortunately, you've got to keep feeding the beast."

He knows you can never feed it enough.

He said, "If you let it consume you…it will."

And it did.

"Winning just went so much further above everything else," Urban said when reflecting on his priorities.

He lost himself to the dark side of achievement.

He needed a detox.

In 2010, Urban jumped off the treadmill.

At his press conference, he said, "I'm stepping down as the head football coach at the University of Florida to focus on family and my other interests away from the sidelines."

Urban started a new search.

Looking for Answers

Urban began to look for ways (and for people) that could help him develop a philosophy on how to chase high performance without losing what's really important to him.

That search led him to Bob Stoops.

Bob was unique.

"There was a time in the coaching profession where having family around—that was a sign of weakness," Urban said. "No one would really say it."

He added, "It was like a medal of honor to say, 'I slept in my office five nights a week.' Or, 'I've worked so hard, I missed this.'"

Bob Stoops had a different value system.

He was one of the first coaches that Urban saw who didn't allow the job to get in the way of his family.

Urban said, "I was amazed by that."

As Urban collected his thoughts on how he would handle his next situation differently, the Ohio State job opened up.

He talked the decision over with his family, and here's what happened next:

Urban's daughter Nicki presented him with a contract.

If he was going to take the job, this is how he would earn the family's support.

On the contract were ten things:

1. *Family always comes first*

2. *I will take care of myself and maintain good health*

3. *I will go on a trip once a year with Nicki (at minimum)*

4. *I will not go more than nine hours a day at the office*

5. *I will sleep with my cell on silent*

6. *I will continue to communicate daily with my kids*

7. *I will trust God's plan and not be overanxious*

8. *I will keep the lake house*

9. *I will find a way to watch Nicki and Gigi play volleyball*

10. *I will eat three meals a day*

Urban presented that contract at his Ohio State introductory press conference.

He said, "This was a contract that my kids made me sign before I was allowed to sign a real contract."

Almost a decade later, I asked him to reflect on that. "If you were to reevaluate Nicki's contract, what would you think?"

He said, "It was awesome. So much of it was symbolic."

It hangs in his office as a reminder.

He said, "It takes me back to a time that I want to make sure never happens again."

Urban has systems in place to help regulate what's really important in his life.

How does he do that?

He tells his players and coaches, "Only you can come up with your priorities."

They can't be your parents' priorities.

They can't be your uncles' priorities.

They can't be the fans' priorities.

You have to determine what's important to *you*.

Once you understand that, you have to determine how you are going to invest into that.

And, when you get off track, Urban says, "You have to have a way of bringing everything back when things start to get chaotic."

The life of a coach is chaotic.

Urban has times in his schedule that are "absolutely off-limits."

What does that look like?

> Mornings: 6 a.m. Group Bible Study
> Noon: Workout
> Evenings: Family Time

His routine has become deeply habitual.

Urban said, "If I fail to keep it going, I can feel myself not staying on track."

He's woven into his life what's really important while still winning 90% of his games at Ohio State.

Societal Reinforcement

When I asked him, "Why do you think coaches think, *I can't do that and still win at a high level?*"

"I've been there," Urban said. "Because of the paranoia of being outworked."

And the environment can reinforce that.

Let's flash back to Urban's resignation speech at Florida.

Urban said, "I'm stepping down as the head football coach at the University of Florida to focus on family."

When he steps down, who steps in?

Will Muschamp.

At the hiring press conference, Will said, "I want to thank my wonderful wife, Carol."

As she stood up, the people in the room applauded her.

Will went on to say, "During the season, she's a widow."

She's dealing without Will a lot because, he said, "I'm very driven in what we do."

Adding, "I think I have an obligation to do that."

When I shared that story with Urban, he grinned and said, "I've been there."

He experienced that same obligation to put his family second so he could chase achievement.

Think about this:

What's Important to Urban

Faith

Family

Health

Society Scorecard

Wins / Losses

Championships

Rankings

Three questions for you:

1. Which side does the fanbase care more about?
2. Which side does the media care more about?
3. Which side does your administration care more about?

If you're like most, you're picking the society scorecard.

But what does that show?

You have to fight for what's important to you.

To do that, detachment from approval becomes essential.

Detaching from Approval

I asked Urban, "Do you think that you've detached from man's approval?"

He said, "To a degree, I have."

Urban doesn't seek outside approval as much as he used to.

I asked him, "When did that shift occur?"

He said, "When I left Florida."

How'd it happen?

Urban filtered what registers on the hierarchy of what's important to him.

He's gone from having an audience of many to an audience of One.

And he has visual reminders everywhere to help with this.

Like these, which hang in the team room:

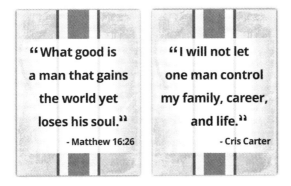

"What good is a man that gains the world yet loses his soul."
- Matthew 16:26

"I will not let one man control my family, career, and life."
- Cris Carter

Urban's insulated himself with routines, reminders, and people to help him stay centered and aligned with what's really important.

ALIGNMENT

PART III

What's Important to You?
List your top five priorities (from page 41) and two intentional investments to support them.

1. ....
    Two intentional investments

2. ....
    Two intentional investments

3. ....
    Two intentional investments

4. ....
    Two intentional investments

5. ....
    Two intentional investments

Who Are Your Thinking Partners?

List five people:

What do they reinforce?

	Society Scorecard	What's Important to You
1.	☐	☐
2.	☐	☐
3.	☐	☐
4.	☐	☐
5.	☐	☐

What are some questions you could ask them to help you navigate what's really important?

BOB STOOPS

Football: Oklahoma (Retired)

Hitting Quick

Bob Stoops is a Hall-of-Fame football coach who spent eighteen years leading the Oklahoma Sooners.

In just two years at the helm, he resurrected the program.

In 2000, his second year as head coach, Bob led the Oklahoma Sooners to an undefeated season and the BCS National Championship.

He hit quick.

Which is why I wanted to show him an interview that Graham Norton did with Matt Damon.

I wanted to see how Bob processed it.

Matt Damon was 27 years old when he won an Oscar for *Good Will Hunting*.

When you hit that early, depending on how you process the success, it can be an incredible perspective-shifter.

That was the case for Matt Damon.

Graham Norton asked Matt Damon to reflect on the night he won his Oscar. Graham asked, "Did you go crazy?"

Matt responded, "Actually, I remember very clearly going back with my girlfriend at the time, and we went to her house, and she went to sleep."

Matt couldn't sleep.

He was alone, thinking.

An emotional rush followed.

At that moment, he learned an important lesson about achievement, saying, "It can't fill you up. If that's a hole that you have, that won't fill it."

Matt felt blessed to learn that at a young age, because, as he said, "I wouldn't have known it unless I knew."

He had to experience the achievement (winning an Oscar) to realize how much the award is overvalued.

That night, Matt played the "what-if" game with himself.

He imagined chasing that achievement his whole life and finally getting the Oscar when he was old.

He said, "My heart broke for a second. It's like I imagined another one of me, an old man, kind of going like, 'Oh my God, where did my life go? What have I done?'"

Bob's Take

I asked Bob if he could relate to Matt Damon's experience.

He immediately said, "I know exactly what he's speaking about."

Bob had the exact same experience in 1996, when he was the defensive coordinator at the University of Florida.

Florida won the national championship that year.

The staff and team celebrated until 7:30 a.m.—at which point, Bob and his wife made it back to the hotel room.

He said, "She went straight to sleep." (Just like Matt Damon's girlfriend.)

Which left Bob to himself…to think.

Bob explained, "I had almost this sinking feeling of, 'Wow, it's over. And it wasn't that big of a deal.'"

It took that experience for him to realize *it's not that big of a deal.*

That realization helped Bob deal with a similar moment four years later, when he won the national championship as head coach of Oklahoma.

Bob said, "I was ready for it this time. Up all night, I remember walking into our room sometime early in the morning and realizing, 'It's gone. The fun is over.'"

He became aware of how fleeting the feeling of achievement is early in his career.

He wasn't going to be the coach that said, "Oh my God, where did my life go? What have I done?"

You Light the Fire

Once you accomplish the "ultimate achievement," something else happens.

I asked Bob, "What do you think of this line: **You light the fire that burns you**."

He said, "That's exactly right."

He added, "I would have been a lot better off losing the first two or three national championships and winning it my third or fourth time."

Fanbases accept progress.

But when you deliver them a championship, what do they now expect moving forward?

Championships.

You set the bar.

Bob said, "Everybody thought I made it look easy when we went undefeated in our second year. And now, that's all the monster wanted."

In college football, the regular season is the playoff season.

The only way to guarantee yourself a shot at the championship is to be perfect and go undefeated.

One loss can prevent you from being one of the teams selected to compete for the national championship.

Fanbases get into that.

I asked Bob to give an example of how intense the Oklahoma fanbase can be.

Bob said, "We lost a game here against Kansas State. I come out to go to the office Sunday morning about six in the morning, and I notice a 'For Sale' sign in my yard."

What's that show?

An engaged fanbase.

Bob will acknowledge that the intensity of the fanbase is part of what makes the University of Oklahoma special. He has great perspective on that.

But fans can lack perspective.

The fanbase's relationship with the coach is conditional on whether or not their expectations are met.

Bob had to manage championship expectations from year two on.

That's sixteen years.

The only way to do that is to detach from man's approval.

The Decision

It's June of 2017. Out of nowhere, after eighteen years, Bob Stoops steps down as head coach of the Oklahoma Sooners.

His decision left everybody (including the athletic director) surprised.

Why?

Bob couldn't talk about his decision with anybody, because as soon as he did, what would happen?

It would leak.

This shows how isolating his job can be.

Bob is an icon.

His decision to leave was an internal experience, and he had to find out what was right for him.

Once he did, guess what happened?

Bob said, "Several tried to talk me out of it."

But he stayed firm with his decision.

I showed him a picture from his press conference when he formally stepped down.

2017 Resignation

I asked him, "When you see this picture, what's the emotion?"

He said, "I was excited about it. I was not solemn whatsoever. I think just because of so many people speaking, it becomes that."

Bob's primary concern was his team.

He met with them earlier in the day—they gave him a standing ovation.

Bob said, "That made me feel great."

The team trusted Bob (and Lincoln Riley, who'd be replacing him) with the direction of the program.

The Timing of the Decision

What can we learn about the timing of Bob's decision?

Returning quarterback Baker Mayfield was the front-runner for the Heismann Trophy. (He went on to win the award and become the number one NFL draft pick.)

With Baker's leadership and the surrounding talent, people close to the program knew how special the upcoming year could be.

Bob had a choice:

1. He could return and have an opportunity to win another national championship to add to his legacy.

2. He could choose a smooth succession.

Bob chose the smooth succession.

It was a mature team.

No one lost their job.

And Bob's successor, Lincoln Riley, led the team to the college football playoffs (semifinals) the following year.

Exiting the Show

What gave Bob the perspective to walk away?

He and I were talking about the movie *The Truman Show*.

I explained to him why his decision to walk away from coaching reminded me of that movie.

In the movie:

> Truman grew up in a dome.
>
> A community was built around him, and his every move was filmed.
>
> Everything was choreographed.
>
> The whole world was in on it...except for Truman.
>
> As Truman got older, he started to catch on.

Through a series of events, Truman was faced with a choice.

He could stay in a world that was built for him, or he could walk through the door into the unknown.

He was the most famous person in the world.

Truman was faced with a choice to walk away from what people wanted him to do in order to find his "true man."

In the movie, Truman did that.

In real life, Bob Stoops did that. He walked away from the Sooner Show.

Not many coaches are able to walk away from a team with a chance to compete for a national championship.

I asked Bob, "What were the top five events that helped shape the perspective that allowed you to walk away from the show?"

Here's what came to his mind.

Five Events That Shaped Bob's Perspective

Ron Stoops Sr.
1934 - 1988

1. His Father's Death

Bob's dad passed away on the sidelines coaching a game against his son (Bob's brother). His dad was 54 years old.

Bob called it a reality check.

As he reflected, he said, "This is how God works."

Bob was working as a graduate assistant at his alma mater, the University of Iowa, when he was offered his first assistant coaching job at Kent State.

Kent State was only 45 minutes from where Bob grew up.

His parents were still living there.

He was only there for nine months.

Those nine months turned out to be his father's last nine months.

Bob was able to be near his father at the end of his life.

Death is a great teacher. It reminds us of what's important in life.

2. The Children's Hospital

Starting in his second year, Bob cleared space in his calendar to visit the tenth floor of the local children's hospital once a week.

He asked himself, "Where can I make the biggest impact?"

He kept his hospital visits quiet because he didn't want the media to grab it.

He was looking for community, but he found perspective.

Touchdowns don't seem nearly as important when you're around someone who is able to have a positive outlook on life despite not knowing whether or not they are going to see tomorrow.

That had a profound impact on Bob. Each visit, he saw what real strength looked like.

3. His Father's Example

Bob's dad coached high school baseball and football for twenty-eight years.

At the height of his career, he was making $40,000.

He wouldn't have traded money for minutes.

Bob swore, "My dad would have never traded me jobs."

He didn't want that lifestyle.

Bob watched him balance faith and family while being a tremendous competitor.

Bob saw that you could do both.

You could balance faith, family, and sport *and* have a huge impact on your players and community.

This would serve as an incredible reference point that would be validated just a few stops down the road in Gainesville, Florida.

 4. Steve Spurrier

Steve Spurrier watered the seeds Bob's father planted. Steve proved that you could win at a high level with a balanced approach.

Bob recalled an event that happened his first year at Florida.

The team had a bye week before playing against Peyton Manning and the Tennessee Volunteers.

At that point in his career, it was the biggest game that Bob had ever coached in.

Here's what Bob did on his off weekend.

After practice on Thursday, Steve Spurrier and Bob Stoops drove to the beach to meet their wives.

They spent the weekend there.

Bob said, "We're floating around in the ocean, and he (Spurrier) says, 'Bobby, you think Phil Fulmer (former Tennessee football coach) is in the ocean today?'"

Bob laughed. "I can't believe I am."

The Gators went on to win the next weekend.

That story captures Steve Spurrier's ability to strike balance while achieving at a Hall-of-Fame level.

He knew that a fresh coach was a better coach.

 5. Childhood Lesson

As we mentioned earlier, Bob's dad was making $40,000 per year.

Meanwhile, his mom worked as a school secretary to help make ends meet.

Bob's parents raised six kids in a little A-frame, three-bedroom home in Youngstown, Ohio.

Brothers in one room, sisters in the other.

Bob shared a room with his three brothers—four guys to one room.

When I asked him what that experience taught him, he said, "I realized **how little I needed to be happy**."

Bob was socialized to understand happiness isn't attached to achievement, money, or status.

That helped shape his perspective.

Bob knew he didn't *need* the job.

He could coach from a place of detachment and trust his instincts despite anything the world had to say.

The Conscious Coach

All of those early experiences helped Bob "The Person" detach from Bob "The Coach."

Which isn't always easy to do—especially when society sees you as Bob "The Coach."

Here's an example that illustrates Bob's ability to detach.

One Friday, Bob's administrative assistant came into his office to have him sign memorabilia (part of their weekly routine).

Out of nowhere, as he was signing, he asked her, "Who is Bob Stoops anyway?"

Bob knew the guy signing the football wasn't his true self.

He was playing a role that people needed him to play.

And it was time for that role to come to an end.

A year after Bob retired, the University of Oklahoma hosted a retirement tribute.

They unveiled this statue:

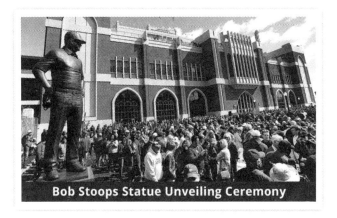

Bob Stoops Statue Unveiling Ceremony

I asked Bob, "When you see that, what do you see?"

Bob said, "That other guy."

Bob saw Bob "The Coach." Not Bob "The Person."

Because he was detached, he was able to see himself in a more objective way.

He shared a story with me that symbolizes how he arrived at his decision to walk away.

It's a story about a strong, faithful Christian:

> He's drowning in a river, and he's praying to God.
>
> He's thinking, "Surely God will save me. He's not going to let me perish in this river."
>
> And while he's sitting there—there goes a log.
>
> There goes something else.
>
> And...something else.
>
> In the meantime, he drowns.
>
> He gets to heaven and he's mad at God. He asks God, "Why didn't you save me? I've been faithful."
>
> "You've got to help yourself at some point. I put a log in front of you," God said. "Why didn't you save yourself?"

The moral of the story: When things come to you, pay attention to them.

Thoughts started to come to Bob.

He asked himself, "What if I stepped down?"

Bob paid attention to that thought and realized it was coming up more and more.

He started to analyze, "Why is that thought coming to my mind?"

It became clear to him that it was the perfect time to step away.

Bob had the right successor in place.

He had a mature team that could handle the transition.

And no one on the staff would lose their job.

He interpreted the signs and wasn't going to allow the opportunity to pursue his true self float by.

He wasn't going to be the guy that drowned in the river.

Bob decided it was the perfect time for him to leave the show.

Reflections: What's Really Important

When things end, it's easier to see them more clearly. That space allows for reflection.

I asked Bob, "How did society measure your success as a coach?"

Here's how he answered.

Society Scorecard:

Wins / Losses
Championships
Players at Next Level
All-Americans
Rivalry Games

When I asked Bob, "What's important to you?"

Here's how he answered.

What's Important to You?

Family
Happiness
Faith
Health
Friends

Then I showed him his lists side by side:

What's Important to Bob	Society Scorecard
Family	Wins / Losses
Happiness	Championships
Faith	Players at Next Level
Health	All-Americans
Friends	Rivalry Games

I asked him, "What do you think?"

He recognized there wasn't a lot of crossover.

One of the best statements Bob can say about his eighteen-year tenure at Oklahoma is, "I didn't lose what's important to me chasing that other stuff."

Yet he still achieved that "other stuff":

> 79.8% Career Winning Percentage
> 1 BCS National Championship
> 10 Big-12 Championships
> 83 NFL Players
> 135 All-Americans

Bob achieved at a Hall-of-Fame level while keeping what was important to him intact.

How'd he do it?

Bob's Healthy Habits

I asked Bob to share a few ideas on how he was able to integrate what's important to him with his job.

Here are a few things that came to mind:

☑ *New Year's Eve*

Bob got this idea from his time with Steve Spurrier.

At the end of the summer, before the team started two-a-days, the staff had a New Year's Celebration.

The coaches were counting on being busy December 31.

That's when all of the best bowl games are.

The men got in coats and ties, their wives wore cocktail dresses, and as Bob said, "We had a big time."

It was a great way to initiate a family-friendly environment at the beginning of the year while communicating a unified expectation.

☑ *Family Night*

Bob said that on Wednesdays, "We had our wives and children all come to the end of practice."

After practice, the staff would have a family dinner before reviewing the film from practice that day.

This was a way to integrate family and create space for quality time.

Bob said, "The children felt like they became cousins to a degree."

When you're around each other's families, it deepens connection and helps reinforce what's important.

☑ *Take Your Kids to School*

Picture Bob Stoops singing with his daughter on the way to school.

For the first sixteen years of their lives, Bob took his kids to school.

He said, "Coaches love to brag, 'I was in the office at 5:00 a.m.'"

Bob had an alternate stance. "I believe that time in the morning shows them how important they are."

The Oklahoma staff didn't start their meetings until 8:45 a.m.—that allowed each staff member an opportunity to start their day with the most important people in their lives.

This is another idea that Bob took from Steve Spurrier.

Bob watched Steve Spurrier take his son to school every day until he was sixteen.

☑ *Children's Hospital Visits*

Bob developed a relationship with a young girl fighting cancer when she was ten years old.

She's twenty-four now.

They still get together for lunch once a year—which speaks to the strength of connection that's formed.

For seventeen years, Bob visited the hospital every week during the season.

The tenth floor of the hospital helped him anchor in to what was important and keep perspective.

☑ *Time with Friends*

When talking about Thursday nights, Bob will say, "Friendships matter."

By Thursday, the work was in for Saturday's game.

Practice usually ended early.

After Bob finished with media requests, he'd connect with friends for an hour to socialize.

☑ *Bring Your Spouse*

When Bob was coming up, wives could only travel to one game a year with the team.

Bob asked himself, "Really? Does that make any sense?"

He knew that nobody was more invested than the spouse.

When he got to Florida, he realized Steve Spurrier shared that opinion.

Steve welcomed the wives on all the away trips.

Bob said, "Ahead of taking the job at Oklahoma, I wanted to make sure that our wives could go to any game."

He negotiated (in his contract) an extra ten seats on the team plane for his assistants to bring their spouses if they chose to.

☑ *Exercise*

When Bob was an assistant at Florida, Steve Spurrier would walk by Bob's office and say, "Bobby, aren't you going to work out today? You need to get down there."

Bob said, "During the season, a lot of coaches don't want you to leave your office."

Spurrier was different. He'd encourage a 45-minute workout for his staff.

Bob took that to Oklahoma, saying, "You have to keep your heart right."

Alignment

Each of these intentional investments allowed Bob to chase high-performance without losing what's really important to him.

His priorities were integrated and aligned with his actions.

Bob wasn't a 24-hour coach.

I asked him, "When they hosted this big tribute for you, what surprised you about the dialogue of everyone as they reflected on their time with you?"

Bob said, "I don't know if it surprised me, but there was no talk of the winning."

What did they talk about?

"The experience and the relationships," Bob said. "That's what lasts."

To be surprised, you must be unaware. Bob was always aware of what's really important.

SUMMARY

PART IV

What's Your Biggest Takeaway from Each Person?

Mike Holder

Mary Wise

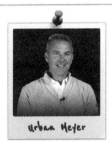

Urban Meyer

Bob Stoops

This Is Our Life

A Summary by Hall-of-Fame Coach,
Sherri Coale

Adapted from the 2018 What Drives Winning conference in Chicago

Mike Holder   Mary Wise   Urban Meyer   Bob Stoops

This Is Our Life
By Sherri Coale
Basketball: Oklahoma

When Brett first asked me the question, "What would you tell your 22-year-old self?"

My immediate answer was, "There's so much."

My next thought was, "I'm not sure I would have listened."

Experience carves capacity.

And when you're a young coach, it's hard to listen, even when you're straining to.

I'm not sure that I could have heard myself, just like that drummer in the movie *Whiplash*.

I cannot imagine a coach on the planet who has watched that movie and not had an absolute visceral reaction.

We watched this drummer passionately pursue greatness.

He's undeniably disciplined and focused—his love for his craft is absolute.

We want him on our team, right?

And then, seemingly while we're blinking, we realize how dark, twisted, and narrow his perspective becomes.

The shift is really subtle.

It's like that exercise that we've all done.

Where we look at the sketch of the beautiful lady—and you look at it long enough and it becomes the craggily old woman.

Once you see it, you can only see the ugly.

That's kind of what happened to the drummer in *Whiplash*.

I remember when I was watching the break-up scene in the movie theatre.

I'm looking at the screen, and I just want to scream at him, "I wish you could hear yourself."

But the drummer's slide to the wasteland was so obvious to everybody…except him.

"If youth knew. If age could."

Mike Holder

Mike Holder's coaching career was filled with unprecedented achievement and irreversible regret.

But what stuck out to me most about Mike was that he *allowed* the journey to give him perspective.

His comment about "leaving a few on the table" because he sometimes "made it too hard" resonates.

Nobody wants to be 'that guy.'

It's easy to see why Coach Holder anchors in to the conundrum: "If youth knew. If age could."

He not only sees the impossibility of that arrangement—he feels it.

The "ifs" are what make it so profound.

Now, on the back side of the ride, he holds a unique perspective: the price and the prize of the journey.

Mary Wise

Mary Wise said that she saw herself as a failure.

She's among the top 2% of her peers in her sport.

She saw herself as a failure because of the lens that she looked through.

If that doesn't cause us to pause for a second and pay attention, I'm not sure what will.

Because if that can happen to Mary Wise, that can happen to anybody.

Perspective is hard to get, and it's slippery to hold.

Urban Meyer

Urban Meyer said, "I became the man that I didn't want to be."

He was sitting in the high seat, but his feet didn't touch the ground.

As a result, he had a breakdown.

He recognized the difference between those two definitions of success.

The discipline necessary to bridge that gap is immense.

You know what Coach Meyer did?

He leaned on his natural inclinations.

He did what coaches do best: He made a practice plan, complete with time increments that would not waver.

He posted signs around his office and around the football complex that reminded him of the man that he wanted to be.

What Urban Meyer did was build a strategy to save him from himself.

Bob Stoops

Bob Stoops' path was more evolutionary.

Coach Stoops is a legend on our campus for his balance.

I can remember years ago saying, "When I grow up, I want to be like Bob."

I wanted to be like Bob because he doesn't ever seem busy.

There was an absence of internal conflict with Coach Stoops.

He was following an example planted by his father and watered by Steve Spurrier.

And because of his parallel walk with his value system, his path was as natural as breathing.

You heard him talk about his trips to the Children's Hospital.

He was searching for community, but he found perspective.

On the surface, that sounds really lucky.

I've got to tell you, Bob Stoops taught me to listen for luck.

He was always aware enough to allow himself to be pulled by the most important things.

So why do we choose this profession in the first place?

What is it that makes us get into coaching?

For most of us, I think the reason is very noble.

We want to make a difference—we want to make an impact.

And yet nobody really tells us about the invisible dragons or the camouflaged sinkholes along the way.

We just go to work.

And then we do well.

Somebody hands us some scissors to cut down a net.

Or they give us a trophy.

And suddenly it's never enough.

The siren song of perfection lures us so softly that we don't even know we're being sung to.

And we wake up and realize that even winning doesn't satisfy what we really need—whatever that need is.

This vortex makes us dizzy.

And we get confused.

It's like the wacky hall of mirrors where everything you see gets distorted, especially yourself.

The suction of expectation guts us.

The environment can get so dark and the tunnel so straight and narrow that we can't see the poor decisions that we might be making.

And we sure can't see the consequences that can grow from those.

Ultimately, what these giants in their respective sports have showed us is that we have to fight constantly for a clear lens.

The championships they win have been so well documented by the world.

But these coaches gave us a little glimpse into the internal struggle of what to do with it all.

When I first did the "What's Important To You?" exercise, I was at a head coaches roundtable.

When you compare what you value to what society values, it's absolutely ludicrous.

You look at it, and it's silly.

I was partnered with a coach who had won multiple national championships.

She sat across the table from me.

When she finished making her list, she put her pencil down and said, "What are we doing? Seriously? *Like, this is our life?*"

And we both laughed.

That empathetic, deep belly laugh that comes when you experience the exact same feeling at the exact same moment.

And then our eyes locked, and they were glassy, and neither one of us dared blink for fear of the water spilling because we knew: *This is our life*.

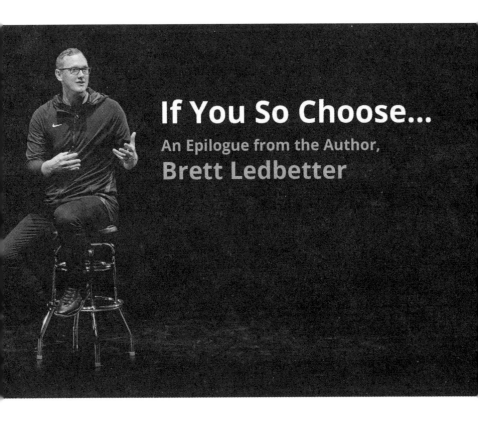

If You So Choose...

An Epilogue from the Author,
Brett Ledbetter

If You So Choose...
By Brett Ledbetter

I was challenged to sum up all the conversations that I had preparing this project. Here's where I landed:

You have to fight just as hard to seek perspective as you do to win a championship.

Society either shapes or distorts what you value.

It starts when you're young.

When you score, what happens?

People applaud.

When you win, people praise.

When you lose, people express disappointment.

What's happening?

A value system is taking form.

You're learning what society values.

If you come from a house where your parent(s) are emotionally attached to your performance, they're mirroring what society values—you're taking cues from them on what's important.

In that case, it aligns with society, and you chase that… because that's all you know.

If you come from a house where your parents are trying to shape you against what society values, you feel in constant conflict—because every time you walk out of the front door, you see something different.

In that case, you want to believe them, but you're confused, because everywhere you look, you're confronted with what society values.

If man's approval is important to you, you become a product of what he values.

You sacrifice what's really important to be successful.

When you do that, you're labeled as committed, driven, or someone who possesses the right mindset.

You start to derive your confidence from that reinforcement.

You learn what it takes to be great.

Then, you take that information into your profession.

You work and you work because that's what the system rewards.

That's how you get recognized and set yourself apart.

The profession turns you into a 24-hour coach.

Eventually, you get your shot.

And you remember what got you there—WORK.

You direct your drive at what the system rewards:

Winning.

You become consumed.

The important people in your life become number two—a long way back from number one.

And what happens?

You win.

Applause.

People praise.

And you feel the love.

You have to keep up the good work.

You work harder and harder to outdo your last performance.

Each time you do, that praise turns into expectation.

Eventually you set the bar so high, you don't know if you can reach it.

And then you don't.

People express disappointment.

You become confused.

It's like they've forgotten how much you've done.

You start to work harder and harder to appease them.

It starts to seem like whatever you do, it's never enough.

Eventually you realize, this is how you're spending your life on Earth.

A major internal conflict starts to develop.

You start to ask yourself, "Is it worth it?"

You realize that you're asking that question more and more.

Eventually, you get to a place where you look yourself in the mirror, and you answer, "No."

And that's when it shifts.

You start to search.

How did I get so far off track?

What did I value?

Why didn't I make time for what was really important?

What did the people I surrounded myself with reinforce?

That breakdown leads to a breakthrough.

You realize that your choices put you in that situation.

And you feel blessed to have that awareness.

Because you realize...you can do it differently, if you so choose.

Next Steps

Road Map

 1. Identify what's important to you

---

 2. List out two intentional investments that help you align your priorities with your actions

---

 3. Align yourself with people who support what's important to you

---

 4. Self-audit: Develop a set of questions that you can ask yourself on a regular basis to determine if you're on track

Sample Self-Audit Questions

1. On a scale of 1-10, how well are you investing in what's important to you?

   How can you get better?

2. What are the unhealthy habits that take you away from what's important to you?

   How can you replace those with healthy actions?

3. Are you surrounding yourself with people who reinforce what's important to you?

   Who does? / Who doesn't?

4. What's your biggest challenge?

   Who can you talk to about it?

Additional Resources

Additional Resources

Explore these online at WRI.WhatDrivesWinning.com

Movies:

Whiplash (2014)

The Truman Show (1998)

Media:

Jim Carrey: 2016 Golden Globe Award Speech

"Matt Damon Gets Emotional Talking about Winning an Oscar," *The Graham Norton Show* (09/25/2015)

David Foster Wallace: "This Is Water," Kenyon College Commencement Speech (2005)

Articles:

Jackie MacMullan: "What a title will never fix for Steve Kerr and Bob Myers," *ESPN* (2016)

Brandon Sneed: "I'm Not the Lone Wolf," *Bleacher Report* (2016)

Wright Thompson: "Pat Riley's Final Test," *ESPN* (2017)

Wright Thompson: "Pretending to Be Okay," *ESPN* (2018)

Books:

The Way To Love, by Anthony De Mello (1991)

Awareness, by Anthony De Mello (1990)

The Only Way To Win, by Dr. Jim Loehr (2012)

Downloadable Worksheets:

Available at WRI.WhatDrivesWinning.com